This journal belongs to

....

Streams in the Desert®

A DEVOTIONAL JOURNAL

© 2009 by Ellie Claire Gift and Paper Corp. Primarily based on *Streams in the Desert*®, copyright © 1925, 1953, 1965, 1996 by the Zondervan Corporation. Published by permission of Zondervan, Grand Rapids, Michigan.

www.ellieclaire.com

Edited by Joanie Garborg
Designed by Lisa & Jeff Franke

ISBN 978-1-935416-09-8

Printed in China

Streams
in the Desert®

A DEVOTIONAL JOURNAL

L. B. COWMAN

...inspired by life

In the wilderness shall waters break out,
and streams in the desert (Isa. 35:6).

In the pathway of faith we come to learn that the Lord's
thoughts are not our thoughts, nor His ways our ways.
Both in the physical and spiritual realm, *great pressure means*
great power! Although circumstances may bring us into the
place of death, that need not spell disaster—for if we trust
in the Lord and wait patiently, that simply provides the occasion
for the display of His almighty power. "Remember his
marvelous works that he hath done; his wonders and the
judgments of his mouth" (Ps. 105:5).

MRS. CHARLES E. COWMAN

LETTER FROM THE PUBLISHER

Since it was first published in 1925, *Streams in the Desert* has become one of the most beloved and best-selling devotionals of all time. A beautiful and profound treasury of comfort and insight, it has provided encouragement to generations of people facing difficult times and tests of faith.

During a period in her life when L. B. Cowman and her husband, Charles, served as missionaries in China and Japan, and later when he was terminally ill, she collected a rich storehouse of writings that helped to sustain her. The compilation included prayerful meditations, inspirational thoughts, poems, and hymns from a variety of sources, as well as her own essays.

Excerpts from those classic writings are arranged thematically to inspire your own thoughts and reflections as you turn each page of our *Streams in the Desert* journal. Following each passage, numbers in parenthesis correspond with the date where that quotation may be found in the original published devotional.

Although selections are taken from the original edition, we have carefully updated wordings that may have distracted modern readers. Except in poetry and Scripture: pronouns such as *thee* and *thy* have been changed to *you* and *your*; verbs such as *cometh* and *shalt* have been changed to more modern forms; the generic terms *man*, *men*, and *he* have been changed to *person*, *people*, or *they* when referring to both men and women. The vast majority of Scripture quotations are from the King James Version of the Bible; some have been changed to other versions for readability. In all cases, the timeless meaning remains unchanged.

Our prayer is that this *Streams in the Desert* journal will be a companion through the dry and difficult places in your life. May the words you read invite you to come to the waters of the River of Life—and beyond, to their very Source.

Hills and Valleys

But the land that you are going over to possess is a land of hills and valleys, which drinks water by the rain from heaven, a land that the LORD your God cares for. The eyes of the LORD your God are always upon it, from the beginning of the year to the end of the year (Deut. 11:11–12 ESV).

All our supply is to come from the Lord. Here are springs that shall never dry; here are fountains and streams that shall never be cut off. Here, anxious one, is the gracious pledge of the Heavenly Father. If He is the source of our mercies they can never fail us. No heat, no drought can parch that river "the streams whereof make glad the city of God."

The land is a land of hills and valleys. It is not all smooth nor all downhill. If life were all one dead level the dull sameness would oppress us; we want the hills and the valleys. The hills collect the rain for a hundred fruitful valleys. Ah, so it is with us! It is the hill difficulty that drives us to the throne of grace and brings down the shower of blessing. The hills, the bleak hills of life that we wonder at and perhaps grumble at, bring down the showers. (01/01)

N. L. ZINZENDORF

Facts and Feelings

We walk by faith, not by appearance (2 Cor. 5:7 RV).

By faith, not appearance.... God wants us to face facts, not feelings; the facts of Christ and of His finished and perfect work for us.

When we face these precious facts, and believe them because God says they are facts, God will take care of our feelings.

God never gives feeling to enable us to trust Him; God never gives feeling to encourage us to trust Him; God never gives feeling to show that we have already and utterly trusted Him.

God gives feeling only when He sees that we trust Him apart from all feeling, resting on His own Word, and on His own faithfulness to His promise.

Never until then can the feeling (which is from God) possibly come; and God will give the feeling in such a measure and at such a time as His love sees best for the individual case.

We must choose between facing toward our feelings and facing toward God's facts. Our feelings may be as uncertain as the sea or the shifting sands. God's facts are as certain as the Rock of Ages, even Christ Himself, who is the same yesterday, today and forever.

When darkness veils His lovely face
I rest on His unchanging grace;
In every high and stormy gale,
My anchor holds within the veil. (09/26)

Proved by Storms

Let us pass over unto the other side (Mark 4:35).

It is much easier to trust when the sun is shining than
when the storm is raging.

We never know how much real faith we have until it is put to the test in
some fierce storm; and that is the reason why the Savior is on board.

If you are ever to be strong in the Lord and the power of His might,
your strength will be born in some storm. (06/03)

SELECTED

There he proved them (Exod. 15:25).

He wants us to be, not hothouse plants, but storm-beaten oaks;
not sand dunes driven with every gust of wind, but granite rocks
withstanding the fiercest storms. To make us such He must
bring us into His testing room of suffering.

Many of us need no other argument than our own experiences to
prove that suffering is indeed God's testing room of faith. (08/28)

J. H. McC

Fear not that the whirlwind shall carry thee hence,
Nor wait for its onslaught in breathless suspense,
Nor shrink from the whips of the terrible hail,
But pass through the edge to the heart of the gale,
For there is a shelter, sunlighted and warm,
And Faith sees her God through the eye of the storm. (04/23)

Wait for God

Blessed are all they that wait for him (Isa. 30:18).

We hear a great deal about waiting on God. There is, however, another side. When we wait *on* God, He is waiting until we are ready; when we wait *for* God, we are waiting until He is ready.

There are some people who say, and many more who believe, that as soon as we meet all the conditions, God will answer our prayers. They say that God lives in an eternal *now*; with Him there is no past nor future; and that if we could fulfill all that He requires in the way of obedience to His will, *immediately* our needs would be supplied, our desires fulfilled, our prayers answered.

There is much truth in this belief, and yet it expresses only one side of the truth. While God *lives* in an eternal *now*, yet He *works* out His purposes in *time*. A petition presented before God is like a seed dropped in the ground. Forces above and beyond our control must work on it until the true fruition of the answer is given. (09/05)

THE STILL SMALL VOICE

In times of uncertainty, wait. Always, if you have any doubt, wait. Do not force yourself to any action. If you have a restraint in your spirit, wait until all is clear, and do not go against it. (04/19)

In the Stillness

*And after the earthquake a fire; and after the fire a sound
of gentle stillness (1 Kings 19:12 RV margin).*

His is a still, small voice. A still voice can hardly be heard. It must
be felt. A steady, gentle pressure on the heart and mind like the
touch of a morning zephyr to your face. A small voice, quietly,
almost timidly spoken in your heart, but if heeded growing
noiselessly clearer to your inner ear. His voice is for the ear of love,
and love is intent on hearing even faintest whispers. There
comes a time also when love ceases to speak if not responded to,
or believed in. He is love, and if you would know Him
and His voice, give constant ear to His gentle touches. (10/03)

WAY OF FAITH

I do not believe that we have begun to understand the marvelous
power there is in stillness. We are in such a hurry—we must be doing—
so that we are in danger of not giving God a chance to work. You may
depend on it, God never says to us, "Stand still," or "Sit still," or
"Be still," unless *He* is going to do something. (02/05)

CRUMBS

*Drop Thy still dews of quietness,
Till all our strivings cease:
Take from our souls the strain and stress;
And let our ordered lives confess
The beauty of Thy peace. (01/30)*

It's Raining Blessings

*For God has caused me to be fruitful in the land of
my affliction (Gen. 41:52 NKJV).*

*It isn't raining rain for me, it's raining daffodils;
In every dimpling drop I see wild flowers upon the hills.
A cloud of gray engulfs the day, and overwhelms the town;
It isn't raining rain for me: it's raining roses down.*

Perhaps one of God's chastened children is even now saying,
"…The rain of affliction is surely beating down on my soul these days…."

Friend, you are mistaken. It isn't raining rain for you. It's *raining blessing*.
For if you will only believe your Father's Word, under that beating rain
are springing up spiritual flowers of such fragrance and beauty as never
before grew in that stormless, unchastened life of yours….

It isn't raining afflictions for you. It is raining tenderness, love,
compassion, patience, and a thousand other flowers and fruits
of the blessed Spirit, which are bringing into your life such
a spiritual enrichment as all the fullness of worldly prosperity
and ease was never able to produce in your innermost soul. (06/15)

J. M. McC.

Are you craving a spiritual blessing? Open the trenches, and God will
fill them…in the most unexpected places and in the most unexpected ways.

Oh, for that faith that can act by faith and not by sight, and expect
God to work although we see no wind or rain. (12/07)

A. B. SIMPSON

Thankful for the Thorns

Reckon it nothing but joy...whenever you find yourself hedged in by the various trials, be assured that the testing of your faith leads to power of endurance (James 1:2–3 WEYMOUTH).

Through the leaves of every trial there are chinks of light to shine through. Thorns do not prick you unless you lean against them, and not one touches without His knowledge.

The words that hurt you, the letter which gave you pain, the cruel wound of your dearest friend, shortness of money—are all known to Him who sympathizes as none else can and watches to see if, through all, you will dare to trust Him wholly. (01/12)

Therefore I take pleasure in infirmities, in reproaches, in necessities, in persecutions, in distresses for Christ's sake: for when I am weak, then am I strong (2 Cor. 12:10).

George Matheson, the well-known blind preacher of Scotland...said: "My God, I have never thanked You for my thorn. I have thanked You a thousand times for my roses, but not once for my thorn. I have been looking forward to a world where I shall get compensation for my cross; but I have never thought of my cross as itself a present glory. Teach me the glory of my cross; teach me the value of my thorn. Show me that I have climbed to You by the path of pain. Show me that my tears have made my rainbows." (04/08)

Answers to Prayer

My expectation is from him (Ps. 62:5).

Every prayer of the Christian, made in faith, according to the will of God, for which God has promised, offered up in the name of Jesus Christ, and under the influence of the Spirit, whether for temporal or for spiritual blessings, is or will be fully answered....

The answer to prayer may be approaching, though we do not discern its coming. The seed that lies under ground in winter is taking root in order to see a spring and harvest, though it appears not above ground, but seems dead and lost. (06/16)

BICKERSTETH

Likewise the Spirit helps us in our weakness. For we do not know what to pray for as we ought, but the Spirit himself intercedes for us with groanings too deep for words. And he who searches hearts knows what is the mind of the Spirit, because the Spirit intercedes for the saints according to the will of God. (Rom. 8:26-27 ESV).

We can just pour out the fullness of our heart, the burden of our spirit, the sorrow that crushes us, and know that He hears, He loves, He understands, He receives; and He separates from our prayer all that is imperfect, ignorant and wrong, and presents the rest, with the incense of the great High Priest before the throne on high; and our prayer is heard, accepted and answered in His name. (10/31)

A. B. SIMPSON

He Knows the Way I Take

He knows the way I take (Job 23:10 NASB).

Believer! What a glorious assurance! This way of yours—
this, which may be a crooked, mysterious, tangled way—
this way of trial and tears. "He knows it."...

This way, dark to the Egyptians, has its pillar of cloud and fire
for His own Israel. The furnace is hot; but not only can we trust
the hand that kindles it, but we have the assurance that the fires
are lighted not to consume, but to refine; and that when the refining
process is completed (no sooner—no later) He brings His people
forth as gold. When they think Him least near, He is often nearest.
"When my spirit was overwhelmed, then You knew my path."

Do we know of One brighter than the brightest radiance of the
visible sun, visiting our chamber with the first waking beam of
the morning; an eye of infinite tenderness and compassion following
us throughout the day, knowing the way that we take?... (04/22)

It is very easy for us to speak and theorize about faith, but God
often casts us into crucibles to try our gold, and to separate it from
the dross and alloy. Oh, happy are we if the hurricanes that ripple
life's unquiet sea have the effect of making Jesus more precious.
Better the storm with Christ than smooth waters without Him. (08/28)

MACDUFF

Life's Highest Attainment

I have called you friends (John 15:15).

To know Him is life's highest attainment....

The reality of Jesus comes as a result of secret prayer and a personal study of the Bible that is devotional and sympathetic. Christ becomes more real to the one who persists in the cultivation of His presence. (05/29)

⁓

We should not be satisfied until we are brought to this, that we know the Lord Jesus Christ experimentally, habitually to be our Friend: at all times, and under all circumstances, ready to prove Himself to be our Friend. (12/03)

GEORGE MUELLER

⁓

The capacity for knowing God enlarges as we are brought by Him into circumstances which oblige us to exercise faith; so when difficulties beset our path, let us thank God that He is taking trouble with us, and lean hard on Him. (11/03)

⁓

God is ever seeking to teach us the way of faith, and in our training in the faith life there must be room for the trial of faith, the discipline of faith, the patience of faith, the courage of faith, and often many stages are passed before we really realize what is the end of faith, namely, the victory of faith.... When God has spoken of His purpose to do, and yet the days go on and He does not do it, that is truly hard; but it is a discipline of faith that will bring us into a knowledge of God which would otherwise be impossible. (05/12)

See God in Everything

*It is the L*ORD*. Let him do what seems good to him (1 Sam. 3:18 ESV).*

"See God in everything, and God will calm and color all that
you see!" It may be that the circumstances of our sorrows
will not be removed, their condition will remain unchanged;
but if Christ, as Lord and Master of our life, is brought
into our grief and gloom, "HE will compass us about
with songs of deliverance." To see HIM, and to be sure
that His wisdom cannot err, His power cannot fail, His love
can never change; to know that even His direst dealings with
us are for our deepest spiritual gain, is to be able to say, in the
midst of bereavement, sorrow, pain, and loss, "The Lord gave,
and the Lord has taken away; blessed be the name of the Lord."

Nothing else but *seeing God in everything* will make us loving
and patient with those who annoy and trouble us. They will
be to us then only instruments for accomplishing His tender
and wise purposes toward us, and we will even find ourselves
at last inwardly thanking them for the blessings they bring us.
Nothing else will completely put an end to all murmuring
or rebelling thoughts. (09/17)

H. W. SMITH

The Living God

*Daniel, servant of the living God,
has your God, whom you constantly serve,
been able to deliver you from the lions? (Dan. 6:20 NASB).*

How many times we find this expression in the Scriptures,
and yet it is just this very thing that we are so prone to lose
sight of. We know it is written *"the living God"*; but in our
daily life there is scarcely anything practically we so much lose
sight of as the fact that God is *the living God*; that He is now
whatever He was three or four thousand years since; that He has
the same sovereign power, the same saving love towards those
who love and serve Him as ever He had and that He will do for
them now what He did for others two, three, four thousand
years ago, simply because He is the living God, the unchanging
One. Oh, how therefore we should confide in Him, and in
our darkest moments never lose sight of the fact that He is
still and ever will be *the living God!* (01/17)

GEORGE MUELLER

Do you know…how to pray prevailingly? Let sight
give as discouraging reports as it may, but pay no
attention to these. The living God is still in the heavens
and even to delay is part of His goodness. (04/29)

ARTHUR T. PIERSON

God Alone

You servants of the LORD, who by night stand in the
house of the LORD.... The LORD who made heaven
and earth bless you from Zion! (Ps. 134:1, 3 NKJV).

It is easy for me to worship in the summer sunshine when the
melodies of life are in the air and the fruits of life are on the tree.
But let the song of the bird cease and the fruit of the tree fall,
and will my heart still go on to sing?... [Then] I know at
last that I desire not the gift but the Giver. When I can stand in
His house by night I have accepted Him for Himself alone.

GEORGE MATHESON

My goal is God Himself, not joy, nor peace,
Nor even blessing, but Himself, my God. (12/11)

⬦

In some way or other we will have to learn the difference between
trusting in the gift and trusting in the Giver. The gift may
be good for a while, but the Giver is the Eternal Love. (10/05)

F. B. MEYER

"The road is too rough," I said;
"It is uphill all the way;
No flowers, but thorns instead;
And the skies overhead are grey."
But One took my hand at the entrance dim,
And sweet is the road that I walk with Him. (05/08)

Don't Worry

Thou, who hast showed its many and sore troubles,
wilt quicken us again (Ps. 71:20 RV).

Never doubt God! Never say that He has forsaken or forgotten. Never think that He is unsympathetic. He will quicken again. There is always a smooth piece in every skein, however tangled. The longest day at last rings out the evensong. The winter snow lies long, but it goes at last.

Be steadfast; your labor is not in vain. God turns again,
and comforts. (11/19)

SELECTED

❧

You are my King, O God; Command victories for Jacob (Ps. 44:4 NASB).

We are children of the King. In which way do we most honor our divine Sovereign, by failing to claim our rights and even doubting whether they belong to us, or by asserting our privilege as children of the Royal Family and demanding the rights which belong to our heirship? (08/08)

❧

OVERHEARD IN AN ORCHARD

Said the Robin to the Sparrow:
"I should really like to know
Why these anxious human beings
Rush about and worry so?"

Said the Sparrow to the Robin:
"Friend, I think that it must be
That they have no Heavenly Father
Such as cares for you and me." (10/10)

ELIZABETH CHENEY

God's Unfailing Love

The hand of the LORD was upon me there. And he said to me, "Arise, go out into the valley, and there I will speak with you" (Ezek. 3:22 ESV).

God's love being unchangeable, He is just as loving when we do not see or feel His love. Also His love and His sovereignty are co-equal and universal; so He withholds the enjoyment and conscious progress because He knows best what will really ripen and further His work in us. (04/13)

MEMORIALS OF FRANCES RIDLEY HAVERGAL

⁓

At the very heart and foundation of all God's dealings with us, however dark and mysterious they may be, we must dare to believe in and assert the infinite, unmerited, and unchanging love of God. Love permits pain.... Where would be faith, without trial to test it; or patience, with nothing to bear; or experience, without tribulation to develop it? (08/10)

SELECTED

⁓

But what things were gain to me, those I counted loss for Christ (Phil. 3:7).

O Love that wilt not let me go,
I rest my weary soul in Thee,
I give Thee back the life I owe,
That in thine ocean depths its flow
May richer, fuller be. (11/07)

GEORGE MATHESON

The Fellowship of His Suffering

I count all things but loss for the excellency of the knowledge
of Christ Jesus my Lord (Phil. 3:8).

When Jesus asks it, let me tell myself that it is my high dignity to
enter into the fellowship of His sufferings; and thus I am in the
best of company. And let me tell myself again that it is all meant
to make me a vessel fit for His use. His own Calvary has
blossomed into fertility; and so shall mine. Plenty out of pain,
life out of death: is it not the law of the Kingdom? (09/21)

IN THE HOUR OF SILENCE

The cup which my Father hath given me, shall I not drink it? (John 18:11).

The most comforting of David's psalms were pressed out by suffering;
and if Paul had not had his thorn in the flesh we would have missed
much of that tenderness which quivers in so many of his letters.

The present circumstance, which presses so hard against you
(if surrendered to Christ), is the best shaped tool in the Father's
hand to chisel you for eternity. Trust Him, then. Do not push
away the instrument lest you lose its work.

Strange and difficult indeed
We may find it,
But the blessing that we need
Is behind it. (07/19)

Believing Prayer

I give myself unto prayer (Ps. 109:4).

Prayer is the link that connects us with God. This is the bridge that spans every gulf and bears us over every abyss of danger or of need. (11/02)

A. B. SIMPSON

No praying man or woman accomplishes so much with so little expenditure of time as when he or she is praying. If there should arise, it has been said—and the words are surely true to the thought of our Lord Jesus Christ in all His teaching on prayer— if there should arise ONE UTTERLY BELIEVING PERSON, the history of the world might be changed.

Will YOU not be that one in the providence and guidance of God our Father? (06/26)

A. E. McADAM

It has been said that no great work in literature or science was ever wrought by a person who did not love solitude. We may lay it down as an elemental principle of religion that no large growth in holiness was ever gained by one who did not *take* time to be often, and long, *alone with God.* (09/29)

THE STILL HOUR

Beware in your prayer, above everything, of limiting God, not only by unbelief, but by assuming that you know what He can do. Expect unexpected things, *above all* that we ask or think. Each time you intercede, be quiet first and worship God in His glory. Think of what He can do, of how He delights to hear Christ, of your place in Christ; and expect great things. (11/02)

ANDREW MURRAY

Music in the Soul

In me...peace (John 16:33).

Paganini, the great violinist, came out before his audience one day and made the discovery just as they ended their applause that there was something wrong with his violin. He looked at it a second and then saw that it was not his famous and valuable one.

He felt paralyzed for a moment, then turned to his audience and told them there had been some mistake and he did not have his own violin. He stepped back behind the curtain thinking that it was still where he had left it, but discovered that some one had stolen his and left that old second-hand one in its place.

He remained back of the curtain a moment, then came out before his audience and said: "Ladies and Gentlemen: I will show you that the music is not in the instrument, but in the soul." And he played as he had never played before; and out of that second-hand instrument the music poured forth until the audience was enraptured with enthusiasm and the applause almost lifted the ceiling of the building, because the man had revealed to them that music was not in the machine but in his own soul. (09/28)

At His Word

"If you can"! All things are possible for one who believes (Mark 9:23 ESV).

*I simply take Him at His word, I praise Him that my prayer is heard,
And claim my answer from the Lord; I take, He undertakes.*

An active faith can give thanks for a promise, though it is not as yet performed; knowing that God's bonds are as good as ready money. (02/22)

MATTHEW HENRY

❧

*Do as You have said...that Your name may be magnified
forever (1 Chron. 17:23–24 NKJV).*

Every promise of Scripture is a writing of God, which may be pleaded before Him with this reasonable request: *"Do as You have said."* The Creator will not cheat His creature who depends on His truth; and far more, the Heavenly Father will not break His word to His own child.

C. H. SPURGEON

It is the everlasting faithfulness of God that makes a Bible promise "exceeding great and precious."... But since the world was made, God has never broken a single promise made to one of His trusting children. (03/08)

SELECTED

❧

*"For all the promises of God in him are yea [yes], and in him Amen [so be it],
unto the glory of God by us" (2 Cor. 1:20).*

We must depend on the performance of the promise when all the ways leading up to it are shut up. (07/01)

MATTHEW HENRY

His Bow in the Clouds

Moses drew near unto the thick darkness where God was (Exod. 20:21).

Mystery is only the veil of God's face. Do not be afraid to enter the cloud that is settling down on your life. God is in it. The other side is radiant with His glory. "Think it not strange concerning the fiery trial which is to try you, as though some strange thing happened to you; but rejoice, seeing that you are partakers of Christ's sufferings." When you seem loneliest and most forsaken, God is near. He is in the dark cloud. Plunge into the blackness of its darkness without flinching; under the shrouding curtain of His pavilion you will find God awaiting you. (03/14)

SELECTED

⸻

Men see not the bright light which is in the clouds (Job 37:21).

The world owes much of its beauty to cloudland. The unchanging blue of the Italian sky hardly compensates for the changefulness and glory of the clouds. Earth would become a wilderness apart from their ministry. There are clouds in human life, shadowing, refreshing, and sometimes draping it in blackness of night; but there is never a cloud without its bright light. "I do set my bow in the cloud!" (05/15)

⸻

If we could see beyond today as God can see;
If all the clouds should roll away, the shadows flee;
O'er present griefs we would not fret.
Each sorrow we would soon forget,
For many joys are waiting yet
For you and me. (07/29)

Faith for Right Now

Lo I am with you all the appointed days (Matt. 28:20, VARIORUM).

*T*he Lord is my shepherd. Not *was*, not *may be*, nor *will be*.
"The Lord is my shepherd," *is* on Sunday, *is* on Monday,
and *is* through every day of the week; *is* in January, *is* in December,
and every month of the year; *is* at home, and *is* in China;
is in peace, and *is* in war; in abundance, and in poverty. (02/08)

J. HUDSON TAYLOR

❦

The land which I do give to them, even to the children of Israel (Josh. 1:2).

*G*od here speaks in the immediate present. It is not something He is
going to do, but something He does do, this moment. So faith
ever speaks. So God ever gives. So He is meeting you today,
in the present moment. This is the test of faith…. The command
in regard to believing prayer is the present tense. "When you pray,
believe that you receive the things that you desire, and you shall
have them." Have we come to that moment? Have we met God
in His everlasting NOW? (02/17)

JOSHUA, BY SIMPSON

❦

When faith goes to market it always takes a basket. (12/29)

Singing All Day Long

When they began to sing and praise, the Lord set ambushments...
and they were smitten (2 Chron. 20:22).

Oh, that we could reason less about our troubles and sing and praise more! There are thousands of things that we wear as shackles which we might use as instruments with music in them if we only knew how.

Those who ponder, and meditate, and weigh the affairs of life, and study the mysterious developments of God's providence, and wonder why they should be burdened and thwarted and hampered—how different and how much more joyful would be their lives, if, instead of forever indulging in self-revolving and inward thinking, they would take their experiences, day by day, and lift them up and praise God for them.

We can sing our cares away easier than we can reason them away. Sing in the morning. The birds are the earliest to sing, and birds are more without care than anything else that I know of.

Sing at evening. Singing is the last thing that robins do. When they have done their daily work, when they have flown their last flight, and picked up their last morsel of food, then on a topmost twig, they sing one song of praise.

Oh, that we would sing morning and evening, and let song touch song all the way through. (05/05)

SELECTED

Peace that Transcends

And the peace of God, which transcends all our powers of thought,
will be a garrison to guard your hearts and minds in Christ Jesus
(Phil. 4:7 WEYMOUTH).

There is what is called the "cushion of the sea." Down beneath the
surface that is agitated by storms, and driven about with winds, there
is a part of the sea that is never stirred.... The peace of God is that
eternal calm which, like the cushion of the sea, lies far too deep down
to be reached by any external trouble and disturbance; and those who
enter into the presence of God become partakers of that undisturbed
and undisturbable calm. (10/20)

DR. A. T. PIERSON

❧

They say that springs of sweet fresh water well up amid the brine
of salt seas; that the fairest alpine flowers bloom in the wildest
and most rugged mountain passes; that the noblest psalms were
the outcome of the profoundest agony of soul. (03/20)

❧

So faith looks up and sails on, by God's great Sun, not seeing one
shoreline or earthly lighthouse or path on the way. Often its steps seem
to lead into utter uncertainty, and even darkness and disaster; but He
opens the way, and often makes such midnight hours the very gates
of day. Let us go forth this day, not knowing, but trusting. (08/23)

DAYS OF HEAVEN UPON EARTH

God of the Impossible

Do you believe that I am able to do this? (Matt. 9:28 NKJV).

We never know where God hides His pools. We see a rock, and we cannot guess it is the home of the spring. We see a flinty place, and we cannot tell it is the hiding place of a fountain. God leads me into the hard places, and then I find I have gone into the dwelling place of eternal springs. (07/05)

SELECTED

We have a God who delights in impossibilities.

ANDREW MURRAY

God deals with impossibilities. It is never too late for Him to do so when the impossible is brought to Him in full faith by the one in whose life and circumstances the impossible must be accomplished if God is to be glorified.... God can "restore the years that the locust has eaten" (Joel 2:25); and He will do this when we put the whole situation and ourselves unreservedly and believingly into His hands. Not because of what we are, but because of what He is. God forgives and heals and restores. He is "the God of all grace." Let us praise Him and trust Him. (11/22)

SUNDAY SCHOOL TIMES

Difficulty is the very atmosphere of miracle—it is miracle in its first stage. If it is to be a great miracle, the condition is not difficulty but impossibility. (10/14)

It Takes Time

And he shall bring it to pass (Ps. 37:5).

It takes God time to answer prayer. We often fail to give God
a chance in this respect. It takes time for God to paint a rose.
It takes time for God to grow an oak. It takes time for God to
make bread from wheat fields. He takes the earth. He pulverizes.
He softens. He enriches. He wets with showers and dews.
He warms with life. He gives the blade, the stock, the amber
grain, and then at last the bread for the hungry.

All this takes time. Therefore we sow, and till, and wait, and trust,
until all God's purpose has been wrought out. We give God a
chance in this matter of time. We need to learn this same lesson
in our prayer life. It takes God time to answer prayer. (04/18)

J. H. M.

⌘

Be quiet! why this anxious heed
About thy tangled ways?
God knows them all. He giveth speed
And He allows delays.
'Tis good for thee to walk by faith
And not by sight.
Take it on trust a little while.
Soon shalt thou read the mystery aright
In the full sunshine of His smile. (04/19)

⌘

Some things cannot be done in a day. God does not make a sunset
glory in a moment, but for days may be massing the mist out of which
He builds His palaces beautiful in the west. (05/24)

The Grace of Gratitude

And again I say, Rejoice (Phil. 4:4).

It is a good thing to rejoice in the Lord. Perhaps you have
tried this, and the first time seemed to fail. Never mind;
keep right on, and when you cannot *feel* any joy, when there
is no spring, and no seeming comfort and encouragement,
still rejoice, and *count it all joy*. Even when you fall into
diverse temptations, reckon it joy and delight and God will
make your reckoning good. Do you suppose your Father
will let you carry the banner of His victory and His gladness
on to the front of the battle, and then coolly stand back and see
you captured or beaten back by the enemy? NEVER!

Our praise will still open fountains in the desert,
when murmuring will only bring us judgment, and even
prayer may fail to reach the fountains of blessing.

There is nothing that pleases the Lord so much as praise.
There is no test of faith so true as the grace of thanksgiving.
Are you praising God enough? Are you thanking Him for
your actual blessings that are more than can be numbered,
and are you daring to praise Him even for those trials which
are but blessings in disguise? Have you learned to praise Him
in advance for the things that have not yet come? (05/26)

SELECTED

Believe...and You Will See

Then believed they his words; they sang his praise. They soon forgot his works; they waited not for his counsel; but lusted exceedingly in the wilderness, and tempted God in the desert. And he gave them their request; but sent leanness into their soul (Ps. 106:12-15).

Here we read of the children of Israel, "*Then* they believed his words." They did not believe until *after* they saw—when they saw Him work, *then* they believed. They really doubted God when they came to the Red Sea, but when God opened the way and led them across and they saw Pharaoh and his host drowned—"then they believed." They led an up and down life because of this kind of faith; it was a faith that depended on circumstances. This is not the kind of faith God wants us to have.

The world says "seeing is believing," but God wants us to believe in order to see.

C. H. P.

Faith is to believe what we do not see, and the reward of this faith is to see what we believe. (07/24)

AUGUSTINE

We boast of being so practical a people that we want to have a surer thing than faith. But did not Paul say that the promise was, by FAITH that it might be SURE? (Rom. 4:16). (06/14)

DAN CRAWFORD

Dare to Be Definite

*Then Jacob said, "O God of my father Abraham and God of my
father Isaac, the LORD who said to me, 'Return to your country
and to your family, and I will deal well with you'...
Deliver me, I pray" (Gen. 32:9, 11 NKJV).*

Jesus desires that we should be definite in our requests, and that
we should ask for some special thing. "What do you want me to do
for you?" is the question that He asks of every one who in affliction
and trial comes to Him. Make your requests with definite earnestness
if you would have definite answers. Aimlessness in prayer accounts
for so many seemingly unanswered prayers. Be definite in your
petition. Fill out your check for something definite and it will be
cashed at the bank of Heaven when presented in Jesus' Name.
Dare to be definite with God. (03/24)

SELECTED

Prove me now (Mal. 3:10).

The ability of God is beyond our prayers, beyond our largest prayers!
I have been thinking of some of the petitions that have entered into
my supplication innumerable times. What have I asked for? I have
asked for a cupful, and the ocean remains! I have asked for a sunbeam,
and the sun abides! My best asking falls immeasurably short of my
Father's giving, which is beyond all that we can ask. (07/27)

J. H. JOWETT

*All the rivers of Thy grace I claim,
Over every promise write my name.*

In His Steps

By faith Abraham, when he was called to go out into a place which he should after receive for an inheritance, obeyed (Heb. 11:8).

It is by no means enough to set out cheerfully with your God on any venture of faith. Tear into smallest pieces any itinerary for the journey which your imagination may have drawn up. Nothing will fall out as you expect.

Your guide will keep to no beaten path. He will lead you by a way such as you never dreamed your eyes would look on. He knows no fear, and He expects you to fear nothing while He is with you. (04/16)

As soon as the soles of the feet of the priests...shall rest in the waters... the waters...shall be cut off (Josh. 3:13).

Faith that goes forward triumphs. (02/11)

He leads us on by paths we did not know;
Upward He lead us, though our steps be slow,
Though oft we faint and falter on the way;
Though storms and darkness oft obscure the day;
Yet when the clouds are gone,
We know He leads us on. (01/01)

N. L. ZINZENDORF

Trust also in him (Ps. 37:5).

The word *trust* is the heart word of *faith*.... The word faith expresses more the act of the will, the word *belief* the act of the mind or intellect, but trust is the language of the heart. (12/15)

Learn To Be Content

I have learned, in whatsoever state I am, therewith to
be content (Phil. 4:11).

A story is told of king who went into his garden one morning,
and found everything withered and dying. He asked the oak that stood
near the gate what the trouble was. He found it was sick of life and
determined to die because it was not tall and beautiful like the pine.

The pine was all out of heart because it could not bear grapes,
like the vine. The vine was going to throw its life away because it
could not stand erect and have as fine fruit as the peach tree.
The geranium was fretting because it was not tall and fragrant like
the lilac; and so on all through the garden.

Coming to a heart's-ease, he found its bright face lifted as cheery as
ever. "Well, heart's-ease, I'm glad, amidst all this discouragement,
to find one brave little flower. You do not seem to be the least
disheartened." "No, I am not of much account, but I thought that
if you wanted an oak, or a pine, or a peach tree, or a lilac, you would
have planted one; but as I knew you wanted a heart's-ease, I am
determined to be the best little heart's-ease that I can." (01/07)

A Planting of the Lord

Awake, O north wind, and come, O south! Blow upon my garden,
that its spices may flow out (Song of Sol. 4:16 NKJV).

Sometimes God sends severe blasts of trial on His children to
develop their graces. Just as torches burn most brightly when swung
to and fro; just as the juniper plant smells sweetest when flung into
the flames; so the richest qualities of a Christian often come out
under the north wind of suffering and adversity. Bruised hearts
often emit the fragrance that God loves to smell. (08/06)

Does the plowman keep plowing all day to sow? (Isa. 28:24 NKJV).

Why should I startle at the plow of my Lord that makes the
deep furrows on my soul? I know He is no idle husbandman;
He purposes a crop. (07/03)

SAMUEL RUTHERFORD

Where the end of hope is, there is the brightest beginning of
fruition. Where the darkness is thickest, there the bright
beaming light that never is set is about to emerge.... Our joys
are made better if there is sorrow in the midst of them. And our
sorrows are made bright by the joys that God has planted
around about them. The flowers may not be pleasing to us,
they may not be such as we are fond of plucking, but they are
heart-flowers: love, hope, faith, joy, peace. (04/25)

Don't Worry

Be anxious for nothing (Phil. 4:6 NKJV).

Many Christians live in a state of unbroken anxiety, and others fret
and fume terribly. To be perfectly at peace amid the hurly-burly of
daily life is a secret worth knowing. What is the use of worrying?
It never made anybody strong; never helped anybody to do God's
will; never made a way of escape for anyone out of perplexity.
Worry spoils lives which would otherwise be useful and beautiful.
Restlessness, anxiety, and care are absolutely forbidden by
our Lord, who said: "Take no thought," that is, no anxious
thought, "saying what shall we eat, or what shall we drink,
or what shall we wear?" He does not mean that we are not to
take forethought and that our life is to be without plan or method;
but that we are not to worry about these things. (10/08)

REV. DARLOW SARGEANT

Great, many and varied may be our trials, our afflictions,
our difficulties, and yet there should be no anxiety under any
circumstances, because we have a Father in Heaven who is
almighty, who loves His children as He loves His only-begotten
Son, and whose very joy and delight it is to support and help
them at all times and under all circumstances. (10/13)

GEORGE MUELLER, IN *LIFE OF TRUST*

Waiting in Expectancy

And there was a voice from the firmament that was over their heads,
when they stood, and had let down their wings (Ezek. 1:25).

Do we not sometimes kneel or sit before the Lord and yet feel
conscious of a fluttering of our spirits? Not a real stillness in His
presence…. Oh, how much energy is wasted! How much time is lost
by not letting down the wings of our spirit and getting very quiet
before Him! Oh, the calm, the rest, the peace which come as we
wait in His presence until we hear from Him! (06/17)

❧

It is better to walk in the dark with God than to walk
alone in the light.

THE STILL SMALL VOICE

Cease meddling with God's plans and will. If you touch anything
of His, you mar the work. You may move the hands of a clock to
suit you, but you do not change the time; so you may hurry the
unfolding of God's will, but you harm and do not help the work.
You can open a rosebud but you spoil the flower. Leave all to Him.
Hands down. Thy will, not mine. (03/30)

STEPHEN MERRITT

❧

Speak, Lord, in the stillness,
While I wait on Thee;
Hushed my heart to listen
In expectancy. (09/18)

Longing Fulfilled

Is anything too hard for the LORD? (Gen. 18:14).

Here is God's loving challenge to you and to me today. He wants us to think of the deepest, highest, worthiest desire and longing of our hearts, something which perhaps was our desire for ourselves or for someone dear to us, yet which has been so long unfulfilled that we have looked on it as only a lost desire, that which might have been but now cannot be, and so have given up hope of seeing it fulfilled in this life.

That thing, if it is in line with what we know to be His expressed will… God intends to *do* for us. *"Is anything too hard for the Lord?"* Not when we believe in Him enough to go forward and do His will and let Him do the impossible for us. Even Abraham and Sarah could have blocked God's plan if they had continued to disbelieve.

The only thing too hard for Jehovah is deliberate, continued disbelief in His love and power, and our final rejection of His plans for us. Nothing is too hard for Jehovah to do for them that trust Him. (11/05)

MESSAGES FOR THE MORNING WATCH

In the outward circumstances in which [Abraham] was placed, he had not the greatest cause to expect the fulfillment of the promise. Yet he believed the Word of the Lord, and looked forward to the time when his seed should be as the stars of heaven for multitude. (11/10)

C. H. VON BOGATZKY

Teach Us to Trust

We are troubled on every side (2 Cor. 7:5).

Why should God have to lead us in this way and allow the pressure to be so hard and constant? Well, in the first place, it shows His all-sufficient strength and grace much better than if we were exempt from pressure and trial. "The treasure is in earthen vessels, that the excellency of the power may be of God, and not of us."

It makes us more conscious of our dependence on Him. God is constantly trying to teach us our dependence and to hold us absolutely in His hand and hanging on His care.

This was the place where Jesus Himself stood and where He wants us to stand, not with self-constituted strength but with a hand ever leaning on His and a trust that dare not take one step alone. It teaches us trust. (03/07)

DAYS OF HEAVEN UPON EARTH

For we through the Spirit by faith wait for the hope of righteousness (Gal. 5:5 RV).

You have made waiting beautiful; You have made patience divine. You have taught us that the Father's will may be received just because it is His will. You have revealed to us that a soul may see nothing but sorrow in the cup and yet may refuse to let it go, convinced that the eye of the Father sees further than its own. (07/26)

GEORGE MATHESON

Wayside Inns

*We are made partakers of Christ, if we hold the beginning of our
confidence steadfast unto the end (Heb. 3:14).*

It is the last step that wins; and there is no place in the pilgrim's
progress where so many dangers lurk as the region that lies hard by the
portals of the Celestial City. It was there that Doubting Castle stood.
It was there that the enchanted ground lured the tired traveler to
fatal slumber. It is when Heaven's heights are full in view that hell's
gate is most persistent and full of deadly peril. "Let us not be weary
in well doing, for in due season we shall reap, *if we faint not.*"
"So run, that ye may obtain." (03/05)

*When you go, your way will be opened up before you step by step
(Prov. 4:12 FREE TRANSLATION).*

The voice of the Almighty said, "Up and onward forevermore."
Let us move on and step out boldly, though we walk into the
night and we can scarcely see the way. The path will open as we
progress like the trail through the forest or the alpine pass,
which discloses but a few rods of its length from any single
point of view. Press on! If necessary, we will find even the pillar
of cloud and fire to mark our journey through the wilderness.
There are guides and wayside inns along the road. (07/02)

Draw Near

Be ready by the morning, and come...present yourself there to me on the top of the mountain. No one shall come up with you (Exod. 34:2-3 ESV).

The morning watch is essential.... You cannot expect to be victorious if the day begins only in your own strength. Face the work of every day with the influence of a few thoughtful, quiet moments with your heart and God.... Meet Him alone. Meet Him regularly. Meet Him with His open Book of counsel before you; and face the regular and the irregular duties of each day with the influence of His personality definitely controlling your every act. (03/02)

⁘

He took Peter and John and James, and went up into a mountain to pray. And as he prayed, the fashion of his countenance was altered, and his raiment was white and glistering...they saw his glory (Luke 9:28-29, 32).

Come close to Him! He may take you today up to the mountaintop, for where He took Peter with his blundering, and James and John, those sons of thunder who again and again so utterly misunderstood their Master and His mission, there is no reason why He should not take you. So don't shut yourself out of it and say, "Ah, these wonderful visions and revelations of the Lord are only for special people!" They may be for you! (11/08)

John McNeill

Glorious Harmony

Giving thanks always for all things unto God (Eph. 5:20).

There are many black dots and black spots in our lives, and we cannot understand *why* they are there or *why* God permitted them to come. But if we let God come into our lives, and adjust the dots in the proper way, and draw the lines He wants, and separate this from that, and put in the rests at the proper places; out of the black dots and spots in our lives He will make a glorious harmony. Let us not hinder Him in this glorious work!

C. H. P.

When the musician presses the black keys on the great organ, the music is as sweet as when he touches the white ones, but to get the capacity of the instrument he must touch them all. (07/23)

SELECTED

Sainthood springs out of suffering. It takes eleven tons of pressure on a piano to tune it. God will tune you to harmonize with heaven's keynote if you can stand the strain. (03/04)

Don't let the song go out of your life
Though it chance sometimes to flow
In a minor strain; it will blend again
With the major tone you know.

What though shadows rise to obscure life's skies,
And hide for a time the sun,
The sooner they'll lift and reveal the rift,
If you let the melody run. (05/05)

Delays Are Not Denials

For the vision is yet for the appointed time.... Though it tarries,
wait for it; for it will certainly come, it will not delay (Hab. 2:3 NASB).

It takes a long time...to learn that *delays are not denials*. Ah, there
are secrets of love and wisdom in the "Delayed Blessings Department,"
which are little dreamt of! Men would pluck their mercies green
when the Lord would have them ripe. "*Therefore will the LORD WAIT,*
that He may be gracious to you" (Isa. 30:18). He is watching in the hard
places and will not allow one trial too many; He will let the dross
be consumed, and then He will come gloriously to your help.

Do not grieve Him by doubting His love. No, lift up your head,
and begin to praise Him even now for the deliverance which
is on the way to you, and you will be abundantly rewarded for
the delay which has tried your faith. (07/04)

SELECTED

~

When your God hides His face, do not say that He has forgotten you.
He is only tarrying a little while to make you love Him better; and
when He comes you will have joy in the Lord and will rejoice with
joy unspeakable. Waiting exercises our grace; waiting tries our faith;
therefore, wait on in hope; for though the promise tarries,
it can never come too late. (10/09)

C. H. SPURGEON

Into the Deep

Launch out into the deep (Luke 5:4).

Our needs are to be met in the deep things of God. We are to launch out into the deep of God's Word, which the Spirit can open up to us in such crystal fathomless meaning that the same words we have accepted in times past will have an ocean meaning in them, which renders their first meaning to us very shallow.

Into the deep of the atonement, until Christ's precious blood is so illuminated by the Spirit that it becomes an omnipotent balm, and food and medicine for the soul and body. Into the deep of the Father's will, until we apprehend it in its infinite minuteness and goodness, and its far-sweeping provision and care for us. Into the deep of the Holy Spirit, until He becomes a bright, dazzling, sweet, fathomless summer sea, in which we bathe and bask and breathe, and lose ourselves and our sorrows in the calmness and peace of His everlasting presence. (02/27)

SOUL FOOD

Amid many and varied trials, souls that love God will find reasons for bounding, leaping joy. Though deep calls to deep, yet the Lord's song will be heard in silver cadence through the night. And *it is possible in the darkest hour* that ever swept a human life to bless the God and Father of our Lord Jesus Christ. (03/20)

TRIED AS BY FIRE

Open My Eyes

Elisha prayed, and said, "Lord, I pray, open his eyes that
he may see" (2 Kings 6:17 NKJV).

The Lord cannot do much with a crushed soul, hence the
adversary's attempt to push the Lord's people into despair and
hopelessness over the condition of themselves or of the church.
It has often been said that a dispirited army goes forth to battle
with the certainty of being beaten.... We need to understand more
of these attacks of the enemy on our spirits and how to resist them.
If the enemy can dislodge us from our position, then he seeks to
"wear us out" (Dan. 7:25) by a prolonged siege so that at last we,
out of sheer weakness, let go the cry of victory. (04/04)

I saw HIM in the morning light,
HE made the day shine clear and bright;
I saw HIM in the noontide hour,
And gained from HIM refreshing shower....

I saw HIM when great losses came,
And found HE loved me just the same.
When heavy loads I had to bear,
I found HE lightened every care....

For as each day unfolds its light,
We'll walk by faith and not by sight.
Life will, indeed, a blessing bring,
If we SEE GOD IN EVERYTHING. (09/17)

A. E. FINN

Call on Him

And it shall come to pass, that whosoever shall call on the name of the LORD shall be delivered (Joel 2:32).

Why do not I call on His name? Why do I run to this neighbor and that when God is so near and will hear my faintest call? Why do I sit down and devise schemes and invent plans? Why not at once roll myself and my burden on the Lord?...

I need not ask whether I may call on Him or not, for that word "whosoever" is a very wide and comprehensive one. Whosoever means me, for it means anybody and everybody who calls on God. I will therefore follow the leading of the text, and at once call on the glorious Lord who has made so large a promise....

He who makes the promise will find ways and means of keeping it. It is mine to obey His commands; it is not mine to direct His counsels. I am His servant, not His advisor. I call on Him, and He will deliver. (05/03)

C. H. SPURGEON

I called him, but he gave me no answer (Song of Sol. 5:6).

Christ sometimes delays His help that He may try our faith and quicken our prayers. The boat may be covered with the waves, and He sleeps on; but He will wake up before it sinks. He sleeps, but He never oversleeps; and there are no "too lates" with Him. (07/10)

ALEXANDER MACLAREN

Faith Is the Victory

*For every child of God overcomes the world: and the victorious principle
which has overcome the world is our faith (1 John 5:4 WEYMOUTH).*

Faith can change any situation. No matter how dark it is, no matter
what the trouble may be, a quick lifting of the heart to God
in a moment of real, actual faith in Him will alter the situation
in a moment. God is still on His throne, and He can turn
defeat into victory in a second of time if we really trust Him.

Have faith in God, the sun will shine,
Though dark the clouds may be today;
His heart has planned your path and mine,
Have faith in God, have faith alway. (06/08)

MARSHAL FOCH

*They looked...and, behold, the glory of the LORD appeared
in the cloud (Exod. 16:10).*

Keep looking up—
The waves that roar around thy feet,
Jehovah-Jireh will defeat
When looking up.

Keep looking up—
Though darkness seems to wrap thy soul;
The Light of Light shall fill thy soul
When looking up.

Keep looking up—
When worn, distracted with the fight;
Your Captain gives you conquering might
When you look up. (04/02)

A Song in the Night

Though the fig tree should not blossom, nor fruit be on the vines, the produce of the olive fail and the fields yield no food, the flock be cut off from the fold and there be no herd in the stalls, yet I will rejoice in the LORD; I will take joy in the God of my salvation (Hab. 3:17–18 ESV).

Last night I heard a robin singing in the rain,
And the raindrop's patter made a sweet refrain,
Making all the sweeter the music of the strain.

So, I thought, when trouble comes, as trouble will,
Why should I stop singing? Just beyond the hill
It may be that sunshine floods the green world still....

I have learned your lesson, bird with dappled wing,
Listening to your music with its lilt of spring
When the storm-cloud darkens, then's the TIME to sing. (08/11)

EBEN E. REXFORD

Ice breaks many a branch, and so I see a great many persons bowed down and crushed by their afflictions. But now and then I meet one that sings in affliction, and then I thank God for my own sake as well as theirs. There is no such sweet singing as a song in the night.

HENRY WARD BEECHER

Afflictions cannot injure when blended with submission. (12/03)

Gently Led

I will lead on softly, according as the cattle that goeth before me and the children be able to endure (Gen. 33:14).

We have not passed this way before, but the Lord Jesus has. It is all untrodden and unknown ground to us, but He knows it all by personal experience. The steep bits that take away our breath, the stony bits that make our feet ache so, the hot shadeless stretches that make us feel so exhausted, the rushing rivers that we have to pass through—Jesus has gone through it all before us.... "He knows our frame; he remembers that we are dust." Think of that when you are tempted to question the gentleness of His leading. He is remembering all the time; and not one step will He make you take beyond what your foot is able to endure. (01/03)

FRANCES RIDLEY HAVERGAL

Bind this comfort to your heart, that the Savior has tried for Himself all the experiences through which He asks you to pass; and He would not ask you to pass through them unless He was sure that they were not too difficult for your feet, or too trying for your strength.

This is the Blessed Life—not anxious to see far in front, nor careful about the next step, not eager to choose the path, nor weighted with the heavy responsibilities of the future, but quietly following behind the Shepherd, *one step at a time*. (01/14)

Lift Up Your Eyes

When Peter had come down out of the boat, he walked on the water to go to Jesus. But when he saw that the wind was boisterous, he was afraid; and beginning to sink he cried out, saying, "Lord, save me!" (Matt. 14:29-30 NKJV).

When the Lord calls to you over the waters, "Come," step gladly forth. Look not for a moment away from Him.

Not by measuring the waves can you prevail; not by gauging the wind will you grow strong; to scan the danger may be to fall before it; to pause at the difficulties is to have them break above your head. Lift up your eyes to the hills, and go forward—there is no other way.

Do you fear to launch away?
Faith lets go to swim!
Never will He let you go;
'Tis by trusting you will know
Fellowship with Him. (06/23)

He...guided them by the skillfulness of his hands (Ps. 78:72).

If you go to Him to be guided, He will guide you; but He will not comfort your distrust or half-trust of Him by showing you the chart of all His purposes concerning you. He will show you only into a way where, if you go cheerfully and trustfully forward, He will show you on still farther. (07/31)

HORACE BUSHNELL

Strength for the Trials

I had fainted unless... (Ps. 27:13).

What do you do when you are about to faint physically?
You cannot do anything. You cease from your own doings.
In your faintness, you fall on the shoulder of some strong
loved one. You lean hard. You rest. You lie still and trust.

It is so when we are tempted to faint under affliction. God's
message to us is not, "Be strong and of good courage,"
for He knows our strength and courage have fled away. But it is
that sweet word, "Be still, and know that I am God." (05/10)

❧

I cannot tell how it is that I should be able to receive into
my being a power to do and to bear by communion with God,
but I know it is a fact.

Are you in peril through some crushing, heavy trial? Seek this
communion with Christ, and you will receive strength and be
able to conquer. "I will strengthen you." (11/09)

❧

God knows that you can stand that trial; He would not give it
to you if you could not. It is His trust in you that explains
the trials of life, however bitter they may be. God knows
our strength, and He measures it to the last inch; and a trial
was never given to anyone that was greater than their strength,
through God, to bear it. (11/13)

Be Still and Know

Be still, and know that I am God (Ps. 46:10).

There is in the swiftest wheel that revolves on its axis a place in the very center, where there is no movement at all; and so in the busiest life there may be a place where we dwell alone with God, in eternal stillness. There is only one way to know God. "Be still, and know." "God is in his holy temple; let all the earth keep silence before him."

SELECTED

All-loving Father, sometimes we have walked under starless skies that dripped darkness like drenching rain. We despaired of starshine or moonlight or sunrise. The sullen blackness gloomed above us as if it would last forever. And out of the dark there spoke no soothing voice to mend our broken hearts. We would gladly have welcomed some wild thunder peal to break the torturing stillness of that over-brooding night. "But Your winsome whisper of eternal love…spoke to us. We were listening and we heard. We looked and saw Your face radiant with the light of love. And when we heard Your voice and saw Your face, new life came back to us as life comes back to withered blooms that drink the summer rain." (11/24)

Answered Prayer

Hear what the unjust judge said. And shall God not avenge His own elect who cry out day and night to Him, though He bears long with them? I tell you that He will avenge them speedily (Luke 18:6–8 NKJV).

I do not believe that there is such a thing in the history of God's kingdom as a right prayer offered in a right spirit that is forever left unanswered. (11/17)

THEODORE L. CUYLER

❧

We must keep on *praying* and *waiting* on the Lord, until the sound of a mighty rain is heard. There is no reason why we should not ask for large things; and without doubt we shall get large things if we ask in faith and have the courage to wait with patient perseverance on Him, while in the meantime doing those things which lie within our power to do. (06/05)

SELECTED

❧

Unanswered yet? Faith cannot be unanswered,
Her feet are firmly planted on the Rock;
Amid the wildest storms she stands undaunted,
Nor quails before the loudest thunder shock.
She knows Omnipotence has heard her prayer,
And cries, "It shall be done"—sometime, somewhere. (10/18)

MISS OPHELIA G. BROWNING

❧

Our prayers are God's opportunities. (11/02)

Our Everyday Experience

And the rest, some on boards, some on broken pieces of the ship.
And so it came to pass, that they escaped all safe to land (Acts 27:44).

It is the common idea that the pathway of faith is strewn with
flowers and that when God interposes in the life of His people,
He does it on a scale so grand that He lifts us quite out of the plane
of difficulties. The actual fact, however, is that the real experience
is quite contrary. The story of the Bible is one of alternate trial
and triumph in the case of everyone of the cloud of witnesses
from Abel down to the latest martyr....

God's promises and God's providences do not lift us out of the
plane of common sense and commonplace trial, but it is through
these very things that faith is perfected, and that God loves
to interweave the golden threads of His love along the warp and
woof of our everyday experience. (08/22)

HARD PLACES IN THE WAY OF FAITH

The colored sunsets and starry heavens, the beautiful mountains
and the shining seas, the fragrant woods and painted flowers,
are not half so beautiful as a soul that is serving Jesus out of love,
in the wear and tear of common, unpoetic life. (11/12)

FABER

Hope in God

Why are you cast down, O my soul? (Ps. 43:5 NKJV).

Regarding all our necessities, all our difficulties, all our trials, we may exercise faith in the power of God, and in the love of God.

"Hope in God." Oh, remember this: There is never a time when we may not hope in God. Whatever our necessities, however great our difficulties, and though to all appearance help is impossible, yet our business is to hope in God, and it will be found that it is not in vain. In the Lord's own time help will come....
"For I shall yet praise him." More prayer, more exercise of faith, more patient waiting, and the result will be blessing, abundant blessing. This is how I have found it many hundreds of times, and therefore I continually say to myself, *"Hope in God."* (02/07)

GEORGE MUELLER

Who told you that the night would never end in day? Who told you that the winter of your discontent would proceed from frost to frost, from snow and ice and hail to deeper snow, and yet more heavy tempests of despair? Do you not know that day follows night, that flood comes after ebb, that spring and summer succeed winter? Hope then! Hope ever! for God fails you not.

C. H. SPURGEON

He was better to me than all my hopes;
He was better than all my fears;
He made a bridge of my broken works,
And a rainbow of my tears. (09/25)

More Than Conquerors

*In all these things we are more than conquerors
through him that loved us (Rom. 8:37).*

This is more than victory. This is a triumph so complete that we have
not only escaped defeat and destruction, but we have destroyed our
enemies and won a spoil so rich and valuable that we can thank God
that the battle ever came. How can we be "more than conquerors"?

We can get out of the conflict a spiritual discipline that will greatly
strengthen our faith and establish our spiritual character. Temptation
is necessary to settle and confirm us in the spiritual life. It is like the
fire which burns in the colors of mineral painting, or like winds that
cause the mighty cedars of the mountain to strike more deeply into the
soil. Our spiritual conflicts are among our choicest blessings, and our
great adversary is used to train us for his ultimate defeat. (01/13)

LIFE MORE ABUNDANTLY

*But thanks be to God, who always leads us in triumph in Christ
(2 Cor. 2:14 NASB).*

If there is a great trial in your life today, do not own it as a *defeat*,
but continue, by faith, to claim the victory through Him who is able
to make you more than conqueror, and a glorious victory will soon be
apparent. Let us learn that in all the hard places God brings us into,
He is making opportunities for us to exercise such faith in Him as will
bring about blessed results and greatly glorify His name. (01/18)

LIFE OF PRAISE

Fashioned by God's Hand

The hand of the LORD has done this (Job 12:9 NKJV).

If people would but believe that they are in process of creation and consent to be made—let the Maker handle them as the potter the clay, yielding themselves in resplendent motion and submissive, hopeful action with the turning of His wheel—they would before long find themselves able to welcome every pressure of that hand on them, even when it was felt in pain; and sometimes not only to believe but to recognize the Divine end in view, the bringing of a child to glory.

Not a single shaft can hit,
Till the God of love sees fit. (04/17)

One that is mastered by Christ is the master of every circumstance. Does the circumstance press hard against you? Do not push it away. It is the Potter's hand. Your mastery will come, not by arresting its progress, but by enduring its discipline, for it is not only shaping you into a vessel of beauty and honor, but it is making your resources available.

Not until each loom is silent,
And the shuttles cease to fly,
Will God unroll the pattern
And explain the reason why
The dark threads are as needful
In the Weaver's skillful hand,
As the threads of gold and silver
For the pattern which He planned. (05/06)

A Very Present Help

God is our refuge and strength, a very present help in trouble (Ps. 46:1).

God uses trouble to teach His children precious lessons. They are intended
to educate us. When their good work is done, a glorious reward will come
to us through them. There is a sweet joy and a real value in them.
He does not regard them as difficulties but as opportunities. (09/07)

SELECTED

Why do You stand afar off, O LORD? (Ps. 10:1 NKJV).

We may be sure that He who permits the suffering is with us in it.
It may be that we shall see Him only when the trial is passing;
but we must dare to believe that He never leaves the crucible....
Let us not rely on feeling, but on faith in His unswerving fidelity;
and though we see Him not, let us talk to Him. As soon as we begin
to speak to Jesus as being literally present, though His presence
is veiled, there comes an answering voice which shows that He is
in the shadow, keeping watch over His own. Your Father is as
near when you journey through the dark tunnel as when
under the open heaven! (01/23)

DAILY DEVOTIONAL COMMENTARY

Bearing Your Cross

Whosoever will come after me, let him deny himself,
and take up his cross, and follow me (Mark 8:34).

There are many crosses, and every one of them is sore and heavy.
None of them is likely to be sought out by me of my own accord.
But never is Jesus so near me as when I lift my cross and
lay it submissively on my shoulder and give it the welcome of
a patient and unmurmuring spirit.

He draws close to ripen my wisdom, to deepen my peace, to increase
my courage, to augment my power to be of use to others,
through the very experience which is so grievous and distressing,
and then…*I grow under the load.* (09/14)

ALEXANDER SMELLIE

His disciples said unto him, Lord, teach us to pray…and he said unto them,
When ye pray, say…Thy kingdom come (Luke 11:1-2).

When Jesus gave His all, Himself for us and to us in the holy
extravagance of the Cross, is it too much if He asks us to do the
same thing? No man or woman amounts to anything in the kingdom,
no soul ever touches even the edge of the zone of power,
until this lesson is learned, that Christ's business is the supreme
concern of life and that all personal considerations, however
dear or important, are tributary thereto. (12/14)

DR. FRANCIS

The Time Is Now

A cup of cold water only (Matt. 10:42).

What am I to do? I expect to pass through this world but once.
Any good work, therefore, any kindness, or any service I can
render to the soul of any man or animal let me do it now.

An Old Quaker Saying

The stone you might have lifted
Out of your brother's way,
The bit of heartsome counsel
You were hurried too much to say;
The loving touch of the hand, dear,
The gentle and winsome tone,
That you had no time or thought for,
With troubles enough of your own....

For life is all too short, dear.
And sorrow is all too great,
To suffer our slow compassion
That tarries until too late.
And it's not the thing you do, dear,
It's the thing you leave undone,
Which gives you the bitter heartache,
At the setting of the sun. (07/30)

Adelaide Proctor

Do not pray for easy lives! Pray to be stronger people.
Do not pray for tasks equal to your powers. Pray for powers
equal to your tasks. Then the doing of your work shall be
no miracle, but you shall be a miracle. (08/03)

Phillips Brooks

A Path of Ascension

Have you seen the treasury of hail, which I have reserved
for the time of trouble…? (Job 38:22–23 NKJV).

Our trials are great opportunities. Too often we look on them as great
obstacles. It would be a haven of rest and an inspiration of unspeakable
power if each of us from now on would recognize every difficult
situation as one of God's chosen ways of proving to us His love and
look around for the signals of His glorious manifestations; then,
indeed, would every cloud become a rainbow and every mountain a
path of ascension and a scene of transfiguration. (07/29)

A. B. SIMPSON

As one went up from story to story, the side chambers became wider all
around, because their supporting ledges in the wall of the temple ascended
like steps; therefore the width of the structure increased as one went up from
the lowest story to the highest by way of the middle one (Ezek. 41:7 NKJV).

Not many of us are living at our best. We linger in the lowlands
because we are afraid to climb the mountains. The steepness and
ruggedness dismay us, and so we stay in the misty valleys and do not
learn the mystery of the hills. We do not know what we lose in our
self-indulgence, what glory awaits us if only we had courage for
the mountain climb, what blessing we should find if only we would
move to the uplands of God.

J. R. M.

Too low they build who build beneath the stars. (01/02)

His Unlimited Supply

When you pass through the waters...they will not overflow you
(Isa. 43:2 NASB).

God does not open paths for us in advance of our coming. He does not promise help before help is needed. He does not remove obstacles out of our way before we reach them. Yet when we are on the edge of our need, God's hand is stretched out. (01/06)

~

Each of us may be sure that if God sends us on stony paths He will provide us with strong shoes, and He will not send us out on any journey for which He does not equip us well. (01/25)

ALEXANDER MACLAREN

~

My God shall supply all your need according to his riches
in glory by Christ Jesus (Phil. 4:19).

What a source—"God!" What a supply—"His riches in glory!" What a channel—"Christ Jesus!" It is your sweet privilege to place *all your need* over against *His riches*, and lose sight of the former in the presence of the latter. His exhaustless treasury is thrown open to you, in all the love of His heart; go and draw on it, in the artless simplicity of faith. (05/27)

C. H. M.

~

His love has no limit, His grace has no measure,
His power no boundary known unto men;
For out of His infinite riches in Jesus
He giveth and giveth and giveth again. (08/05)

ANNIE JOHNSON FLINT

Lord, Make It Clear

*Your ears shall hear a word behind you, saying, "This is
the way, walk in it," whenever you turn to the right hand
or whenever you turn to the left (Isa. 30:21 NKJV).*

When we are in doubt or difficulty, when many voices urge this
course or the other, when prudence utters one advice and faith
another, then let us be still, hushing each intruder, calming ourselves
in the sacred hush of God's presence; let us study His Word in
the attitude of devout attention; let us lift up our nature into
the pure light of His face, eager only to know what God the Lord
shall determine—and before long a very distinct impression will
be made, the unmistakable unfolding of His secret counsel. (06/20)

DAVID

We do not know what to do, but our eyes are on you (2 Chron. 20:12 ESV).

*Being in doubt I say,
"Lord, make it plain;
Which is the true, safe way?
Which would be gain?
I am not wise to know,
Nor sure of foot to go;
What is so clear to Thee,
Lord, make it clear to me!"*

It is such a comfort to drop the tangles of life into
God's hands and leave them there. (07/06)

Be Careful for Nothing

Faith is...the evidence of things not seen (Heb. 11:1).

True faith drops its letter in the post office box,
and lets it go. Distrust holds on to a corner of it,
and wonders that the answer never comes....

This is the way with true faith. It hands its case over
to God, and then He works.... Faith is a receiving or
still better, a taking of God's proffered gifts. We may
believe, and come, and commit, and rest; but we will
not fully realize all our blessing until we begin to
receive and come into the attitude of abiding and taking.

DAYS OF HEAVEN UPON EARTH

The command, "Be careful for nothing," is unlimited; and so
is the expression, "casting all your care on him." If we cast our
burdens onto another, can they continue to press in on us? If we
bring them away with us from the throne of grace, it is evident
we do not leave them there. With respect to myself, I have made
this one test of my prayers: if after committing anything to God,
I can, like Hannah, come away and have my mind no more sad,
my heart no more pained or anxious, I look on it as the
proof that I have prayed in faith; but if I bring away my burden,
I conclude that faith was not in exercise. (04/24)

DR. PAYSON

He Intercedes for Us

Watch unto prayer (1 Pet. 4:7).

If Jesus, the strong Son of God, felt it necessary to rise before the breaking of the day to pour out His heart to God in prayer, how much more we ought to pray to Him who is the Giver of every good and perfect gift, and who has promised all things necessary for our good.

What Jesus gathered into His life from His prayers we can never know; but this we do know, that the prayerless life is a powerless life. A prayerless life may be a noisy life, and fuss around a great deal; but such a life is far removed from Him who, by day and night, prayed to God. (06/06)

SELECTED

Seeing then that we have a great high Priest...Jesus, the Son of God, let us hold fast our profession.... Let us therefore come boldly unto the throne of grace, that we may obtain mercy, and find grace to help in time of need (Heb. 4:14, 16).

Our great Helper in prayer is the Lord Jesus Christ, our Advocate with the Father, our Great High Priest, whose chief ministry for us these centuries has been intercession and prayer. It is He who takes our imperfect petitions from our hands, cleanses them from their defects, corrects their faults, and then claims their answer from His Father on His own account and through His all-atoning merits and righteousness. (07/20)

A. B. SIMPSON

Fully Surrendered

You could have no power at all against Me unless it had
been given you from above (John 19:11 NKJV).

Nothing that is not God's will can come into the life of one
who trusts and obeys God. This fact is enough to make our life
one of ceaseless thanksgiving and joy. For "God's will is the one
hopeful, glad, and glorious thing in the world"; and it is working
in the omnipotence for us all the time, with nothing to prevent
it if we are surrendered and believing. (08/14)

H. W. SMITH

Because you have done this thing and have not withheld your son,
your only son...I will greatly multiply your seed as the stars of the heavens
...because you have obeyed My voice (Gen. 22:16-18 NASB).

And from that day to this, people have been learning that when,
at God's voice, they surrender up to Him the one thing above all
else that was dearest to their very hearts, that same thing is returned
to them by Him a thousand times over. Abraham gives up his one
and only son, at God's call, and with this disappear all his hopes for
the boy's life and manhood, and for a noble family bearing his name.
But the boy is restored, the family becomes as the stars and sands in
number, and out of it, in the fullness of time, appears Jesus Christ.

That is just the way God meets every real sacrifice
of every child of His. (07/16)

C. G. TRUMBULL

Showers of Blessings

I will cause the shower to come down in his season;
there shall be showers of blessing (Ezek. 34:26).

What is your *season* this morning? Is it a season of drought?
Then that is the season for showers. Is it a season of great
heaviness and black clouds? Then that is the season for showers.
"As your days so shall your strength be." "I will give you
showers of blessing." The word is in the plural. All kinds of
blessings God will send. All God's blessings go together,
like links in a golden chain. If He gives converting grace,
He will also give comforting grace. He will send "showers
of blessings." Look up today, O parched plant, and open
your leaves and flowers for a heavenly watering. (01/08)

C. H. Spurgeon

Are you in some great trouble? Have you had some great
disappointment, have you met some sorrow, some
unspeakable loss? Are you in a hard place?…
Take your trouble the right way. Commit it to God.
Praise Him that He makes "all things work together
for good," and that "God works for those that wait for him."
There will be blessings, help and revelations of God that will
come to you that never could otherwise have come; and many
besides yourself will receive great light and blessing. (08/25)

C. H. P

Walking in the Dark

Who among you fears the LORD and obeys the voice of his servant?
Let him who walks in darkness and has no light trust in the name
of the LORD and rely on his God (Isa. 50:10 ESV).

What shall the believer do in times of darkness—the darkness
of perplexity and confusion, not of heart but of mind?
Times of darkness come to faithful and believing disciples
who are walking obediently in the will of God; seasons when they
do not know what to do, nor which way to turn. The sky is overcast
with clouds. The clear light of Heaven does not shine on their
pathway. They feel as if they were groping their way in darkness.

Beloved, is this you? What shall believers do in times
of darkness? Listen! "Let them trust in the name of the Lord,
and rely on their God."

The first thing to do is do nothing…. We are to simply trust God.
While we trust, God can work. Worry prevents Him from doing
anything for us…. The peace of God must quiet our minds and rest
our hearts. We must put our hand in the hand of God like a little
child, and let Him lead us out into the bright sunshine of His love.

He knows the way out of the woods. Let us climb up into His arms,
and trust Him to take us out by the shortest and surest road. (10/07)

Dr. Pardington

Count It All Joy

And we know that all things work together for good to them that love God (Rom. 8:28).

How wide is this assertion of the Apostle Paul! He does not say, "We know that *some* things," or "*most* things," or "*joyous* things," but "ALL things." From the minutest to the most momentous; from the humblest event in daily providence to the great crisis hours in grace.

And all things "*work*"—they *are* working; not all things *have* worked, or *shall* work; but it is a present operation. (06/10)

MACDUFF

⊱⊰

Let us lay aside every weight, and the sin which so easily ensnares us, and let us run with endurance the race that is set before us (Heb. 12:1 NKJV).

Let us refuse to be discouraged. Let us refuse to be unhappy. Let us "count it all joy" when we cannot feel one emotion of happiness. Let us rejoice by faith, by resolution, by reckoning, and we shall surely find that God will make the reckoning real. (10/16)

SELECTED

⊱⊰

Your heavenly Father knows (Matt. 6:32 NKJV).

I can still believe that a day comes for all of us, however far off it may be, when we shall understand; when these tragedies that now blacken and darken the very air of heaven for us, will sink into their places in a scheme so august, so magnificent, so joyful, that we shall laugh for wonder and delight. (02/12)

ARTHUR CHRISTOPHER BACON

The Way to Peace

We know not what we should pray for as we ought (Rom. 8:26).

Much that perplexes us in our Christian experience is simply the answer to our prayers. We pray for patience and our Father sends those who tax us to the utmost; for "tribulation works patience."

We pray for submission and God sends sufferings, for "we learn obedience by the things we suffer."

We pray for unselfishness and God gives us opportunities to sacrifice ourselves by thinking on the things of others and by laying down our lives for others.

The way to peace and victory is to accept every circumstance, every trial, straight from the hand of a loving Father; and to live up in the heavenly places, above the clouds, in the very presence of the throne, and to look down from the glory on our environment as lovingly and divinely appointed. (05/13)

SELECTED

❧

So the Lord blessed the latter end of Job more than his beginning (Job 42:12).

There are blessings which we cannot obtain if we cannot accept and endure suffering. There are joys that can come to us only through sorrow. There are revealings of Divine truth which we can get only when earth's lights have gone out. There are harvests which can grow only after the plowshare has done its work. (10/04)

SELECTED

Faith for Desperate Days

Without faith it is impossible to please Him, for he who comes to God must believe that He is, and that He is a rewarder of those who diligently seek Him. (Heb. 11:6 NKJV).

The faith for desperate days.

The Bible is full of such days. Its record is made up of them, its songs are inspired by them, its prophecy is concerned with them, and its revelation has come through them. The desperate days are the stepping-stones in the path of light. They seem to have been God's opportunity and man's school of wisdom. (03/25)

REV. S. CHADWICK

Difficulties and obstacles are God's challenges to faith. When hindrances confront us in the path of duty, we are to recognize them as vessels for faith to fill with the fullness and all-sufficiency of Jesus; and as we go forward, simply and fully trusting Him, we may be tested, we may have to wait and let patience have her perfect work; but we shall surely find at last the stone rolled away and the Lord waiting to render to us double for our time of testing. (11/15)

A. B. SIMPSON

Remember it is the very time for faith to work when sight ceases. The greater the difficulties, the easier for faith; as long as there remain certain natural prospects, faith does not get on even as easily as where natural prospects fail. (11/10)

GEORGE MUELLER

Through a Consecrated Soul

The eyes of the Lord run to and fro throughout the
whole earth, to show Himself strong on behalf of
those whose heart is loyal to Him. (2 Chron. 16:9 NKJV).

"The world is waiting yet to see what God can do through
a consecrated soul." Not the world alone, but God Himself
is waiting for one who will be more fully devoted to Him than
any who have ever lived; who will be willing to be nothing
that Christ may be all; who will grasp God's own purposes;
and taking His humility and His faith, His love and His power
will, without hindering, continue to let God do exploits.

C. H. P.

There is no limit to what God can do with people,
providing they will not touch the glory.

God, God alone became my portion. I found my all in Him;
I wanted nothing else. And by the grace of God this has
remained.... Since that time the revelation He has made
of Himself has become unspeakably blessed to me, and
I can say from my heart, God is an infinitely lovely Being.
Oh, be not satisfied until in your own inmost soul
you can say, God is an infinitely lovely Being! (07/18)

GEORGE MUELLER

The Purpose in Rest

Into a desert place apart (Matt. 14:13).

"There is no music in a rest, but there is the making of music in it."
In our whole life-melody the music is broken off here and there by
"rests," and we foolishly think we have come to the end of the tune....

Not without design does God write the music of our lives. Be it ours
to learn the tune and not be dismayed at the "rests." They are not to
be slurred over, not to be omitted, not to destroy the melody, not to
change the keynote. If we look up, God Himself will beat the time for
us. With the eye on Him, we shall strike the next note full and clear.
If we sadly say to ourselves, "There is no music in a rest," let us not
forget "there is the making of music in it." The making of music is
often a slow and painful process in this life. How patiently God works
to teach us! How long He waits for us to learn the lesson! (01/22)

RUSKIN

I will be as the dew unto Israel (Hos. 14:5).

Dew will never gather while there is either heat or wind.
The temperature must fall and the wind cease and the air come
to a point of coolness and rest—absolute rest, so to speak—before
it can yield up its invisible particles of moisture to bedew either
herb or flower. So the grace of God does not come forth to rest
the soul until the *still point* is fairly and fully reached. (01/30)

After the Rain

He shall come down like rain upon the mown grass (Ps. 72:6).

There is no method of obtaining a velvety lawn but by repeated mowings; and there is no way of developing tenderness, evenness, sympathy, but by the passing of God's scythes. How constantly the Word of God compares people to grass, and His glory to its flower! But when grass is mown, and all the tender shoots are bleeding, and desolation reigns where flowers were bursting, it is the most acceptable time for showers of rain falling soft and warm....

Do not dread the scythe—it is sure to be followed by the shower. (11/11)

F. B. MEYER

The tree that grows where tempests toss its boughs and bend its trunk often almost to breaking, is often more firmly rooted than the tree which grows in the sequestered valley where no storm ever brings stress or strain. The same is true of life. The grandest character is grown in hardship. (10/27)

SELECTED

Nevertheless afterward (Heb. 12:11).

You can always count on God to make the "afterward" of difficulties, if rightly overcome, a thousand times richer and fairer than the forward. "No chastening... seems joyous, nevertheless afterward..." What a yield! (11/29)

When All Else Fails

Let me test, I pray, just once more with the fleece (Judg. 6:39 NKJV).

The first phase of faith believes when there are favorable emotions, the second believes when there is the absence of feeling, but this third form of faith believes God and His Word when circumstances, emotions, appearances, people, and human reason all urge to the contrary. Paul exercised this faith in Acts 27:20, 25, "And when neither sun nor stars in many days appeared, and no small tempest lay on us, all hope that we should be saved was then taken away." In spite of all this Paul said, "Wherefore, sirs, be of good cheer; *for I believe God*, that it shall be even as it was told me."

May God give us faith to fully trust His Word though everything else witness the other way. (07/21)

C. H. P.

❧

Each of three boys gave a definition of faith which is an illustration of the tenacity of faith. The first boy said, "It is taking hold of Christ"; the second, "Keeping hold"; and the third, "Not letting go." (04/29)

❧

*Who against hope believed in hope…and being not weak in faith…
he staggered not at the promise of God through unbelief (Rom. 4:18-20).*

"The only way," [said George Mueller], "to learn strong faith is to endure great trials. I have learned my faith by standing firm amid severe testings." This is very true.
The time to trust is when all else fails. (06/02)

The Fruit of the Storm

And there arose a great storm (Mark 4:37).

Some of the storms of life come *suddenly*: a great sorrow, a bitter disappointment, a crushing defeat. Some come *slowly*. They appear on the ragged edges of the horizon no larger than a man's hand, but trouble that seems so insignificant spreads until it covers the sky and overwhelms us. Yet it is in the storm that God equips us for service…. When God wants to make us He puts us into some storm. The history of mankind is always rough and rugged. None of us is made until we have been out into the surge of the storm and found the sublime fulfillment of the prayer: "O God, take me, break me, make me."… *You* have been in the storms and swept by the blasts. Have they left you broken, weary, beaten in the valley, or have they lifted you to the sunlit summits of a richer, deeper, more abiding manhood and womanhood? Have they left you with more sympathy with the storm-swept and the battle-scarred? (01/16)

SELECTED

The Lord has His way in the whirlwind and in the storm (Nah. 1:3 NKJV).

Have you asked to be made like your Lord? Have you longed for the fruit of the Spirit and have you prayed for sweetness and gentleness and love? Then do not fear the stormy tempest that is at this moment sweeping through your life. A blessing is in the storm, and there will be the rich fruit in the "afterward." (07/28)

HENRY WARD BEECHER

In His Time

Stay there until I bring you word (Matt. 2:13 NKJV).

Oh restless heart…leave God to order all your days. Patience and trust, in the dullness of the routine of life, will be the best preparation for a courageous bearing of the tug and strain of the larger opportunity which God may sometime send you. (03/17)

⁓

When I remember the power of the "still small voice," I will not murmur that sometimes the Spirit suffers me not to go. Teach me to see another door in the very inaction of the hour. Help me to find in the very prohibition a way to serve You, a new opening into Your service. Inspire me with the knowledge that I may at times be called to do my duty by doing nothing, to work by keeping still, to serve by waiting.

GEORGE MATHESON

When I cannot understand my Father's leading,
And it seems to be but hard and cruel fate,
Still I hear that gentle whisper ever pleading,
God is working, God is faithful, ONLY WAIT. (09/24)

⁓

There's a simplicity about God in working out His plans, yet a resourcefulness equal to any difficulty and an unswerving faithfulness to His trusting child and an unforgetting steadiness in holding to His purpose…. It's safe to trust God's methods and to go by His clock. (10/14)

S. D. GORDON

In the Morning

You make the outgoings of the morning and evening
rejoice (Ps. 65:8 NKJV).

Get up early and…watch God make a morning. The dull gray will give way as God pushes the sun towards the horizon, and there will be tints and hues of every shade that will blend into one perfect light as the full-orbed sun bursts into view. As the King of day moves forth majestically, flooding the earth and every lowly vale, listen to the music of heaven's choir as it sings of the majesty of God and the glory of the morning.…

The clear, pure light of the morning made me long for the truth in my heart, which alone could make me pure and clear as the morning, tune me up to the concert-pitch of the nature around me. And the wind that blew from the sunrise made me hope in the God who had first breathed into my nostrils the breath of life; that He would at length so fill me with His breath, His mind, His Spirit, that I should think only His thoughts and live His life, finding there my own life, only glorified infinitely. (11/28)

GEORGE MACDONALD

The Garden of My Heart

My Father is the husbandman (John 15:1).

Many of the richest blessings which have come down to us from the past are the fruit of sorrow or pain. We should never forget that redemption, the world's greatest blessing, is the fruit of the world's greatest sorrow. In every time of sharp pruning when the knife is deep and the pain is sore, it is an unspeakable comfort to read, "My Father is the husbandman."... Pruning seems to be destroying the vine, the gardener appears to be cutting it all away; but he looks on into the future and knows that the final outcome will be the enrichment of its life and greater abundance of fruit. (09/19)

Dr. Miller

God is a wise husbandman, "who waits for the precious fruit of the earth, and has long patience for it." He cannot gather the fruit until it is ripe. He knows when we are spiritually ready to receive the blessing to our profit and His glory. Waiting in the sunshine of His love is what will ripen the soul for His blessing. Waiting under the cloud of trial that breaks in showers of blessings is as needful. Be assured that if God waits longer than you could wish, it is only to make the blessing doubly precious. God waited four thousand years until the fullness of time before He sent His Son. Our times are in His hands; He will avenge His chosen ones speedily; He will make haste for our help and not delay one hour too long. (07/22)

Andrew Murray

The Master's Touch

I will lay your stones with colorful gems (Isa. 54:11 NKJV).

You are still in the quarry and not complete, and therefore to you, as once to us, much is inexplicable. But you are destined for a higher building and one day you will be placed in it by hands not human, a living stone in a heavenly temple.

In the still air the music lies unheard;
In the rough marble beauty hides unseen;
To make the music and the beauty needs
The master's touch, the sculptor's chisel keen.

Great Master, touch us with Thy skillful hands;
Let not the music that is in us die!
Great Sculptor, hew and polish us; nor let,
Hidden and lost, thy form within us lie! (09/01)

Straining, driving effort does not accomplish the work God gives His children to do. Only God Himself, who always works without strain and who never overworks, can do the work that He assigns to His children. When they restfully trust Him to do it, it will be well done and completely done. The way to let Him do His work through us is to partake of Christ so fully, by faith, that He more than fills our life. (09/03)

SUNDAY SCHOOL TIMES

Overcome Where You Are

When you pray, believe (Mark 11:24 NKJV).

You will never learn faith in comfortable surroundings. God gives us the promises in a quiet hour; God seals our covenants with great and gracious words, then He steps back and waits to see how much we believe; then He lets the tempter come, and the test seems to contradict all that He has spoken. It is then that faith wins its crown. That is the time to look up through the storm and among the trembling, frightened seamen cry, "I believe God that it shall be even as it was told me." (01/04)

They overcame him by the blood of the Lamb...and they loved not their lives unto the death (Rev. 12:11).

Do not wait for some ideal situation, some romantic difficulty, some far-away emergency; but rise to meet the actual conditions which the providence of God has placed around you today. Your crown of glory lies embedded in the very heart of these things— those hardships and trials that are pressing you this very hour, week and month of your life. The hardest things are not those that the world knows of. Down in your secret soul, unseen and unknown by any but Jesus, there is a little trial that you would not dare to mention that is harder for you to bear than martyrdom.

There, beloved, lies your crown. May God help you to overcome and sometime wear it. (11/16)

SELECTED

All the Way

Hitherto hath the LORD helped us (1 Sam. 7:12).

He who hath helped thee hitherto
Will help thee all thy journey through.

When read in Heaven's light, how glorious and marvelous a
prospect will your "hitherto" unfold to your grateful eye.

C. H. SPURGEON

This my song through endless ages,
Jesus led me all the way. (12/31)